# Pandemic Baby

Published in the UK in 2021
by Icon Books Ltd, Omnibus Business Centre,
39–41 North Road, London N7 9DP
email: info@iconbooks.com
www.iconbooks.com

Sold in the UK, Europe and Asia
by Faber & Faber Ltd, Bloomsbury House,
74–77 Great Russell Street, London WC1B 3DA or their agents

Distributed in the UK, Europe and Asia
by Grantham Book Services,
Trent Road, Grantham NG31 7XQ

Distributed in Australia and New Zealand
by Allen & Unwin Pty Ltd,
PO Box 8500, 83 Alexander Street, Crows Nest, NSW 2065

Distributed in South Africa
by Jonathan Ball, Office B4, The District,
41 Sir Lowry Road, Woodstock 7925

Distributed in India by Penguin Books India,
7th Floor, Infinity Tower – C, DLF Cyber City,
Gurgaon 122002, Haryana

Distributed in the USA by
Publishers Group West,
1700 Fourth Street, Berkeley, CA 94710

Distributed in Canada by
Publishers Group Canada,
76 Stafford Street, Unit 300, Toronto, Ontario M6J 2S1

ISBN: 978-178578-800-0

Designed and typeset by Nicholas Halliday, HallidayBooks.com

Printed and bound in Great Britain
by Clays Ltd, Elcograf S.p.A.

# Pandemic Baby

Becoming a Parent in Lockdown

## Pia Bramley

# SPRING

Our family is about to change.

But we didn't expect the rest of the
world to change so dramatically too.

We are passengers on this
strange journey together.

There are new reasons to worry,
and new joys.

It's impossible to know
how to prepare.

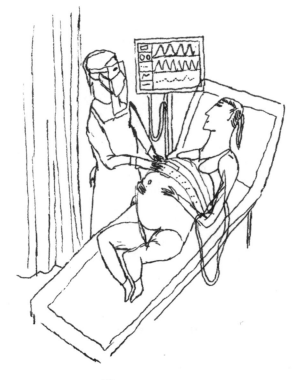

I'm on my own
but when I hear your heartbeat,
I know that I am not alone.

How does it feel to be here?

These first days aren't quite how
we imagined them to be,

but pictures of you transmit a little bit
of brightness into the gloom.

And, I suppose, now that
you're here we'll just have to
keep on going together.

# SUMMER

Every day more cards arrive from
all the people we can't see.

More milk, more news.

We watch the sunny days
pass at a distance,

and elsewhere exists only
on tiny screens.

When we leave the house, you
seem smaller in all this outside space.
Short walks on the quiet streets,

and quickly back home again,

where nothing much changes,
but you seem different every minute.

Navigating through the weather
of your moods, always tired,

always together.

Finding moments of solitude.

# AUTUMN

It's still a surprise,
sometimes, to walk into a
room and see a baby there.

Your wonder brightens
these routines.

But the house seems to
shrink a little each day.

And sometimes the hunt for
distractions can't break a bad mood.

But just as we begin to
feel entirely exhausted,
there are moments of peace.

Thanks to you, we know that even
the most mundane chores

provide a chance for a funny game.

It doesn't feel right
for you to experience the
world through screens,

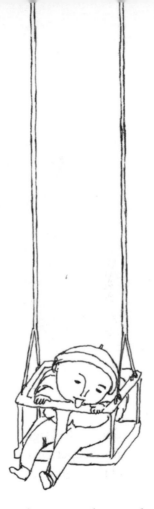

so we let you explore with as
much freedom as we can.

The space between joy and
fury feels very small.

# WINTER

What time is it?

What day of the week?

We're settling into
these new rhythms,

the comfort of repetition.

We can't complain that we
have nothing to do.

There are always new types
of mess to clean up.

Growing out of something,
and into another.

Our same old streets are new to you.

We try to feel as
fascinated by light switches
and radiators as you.

# SPRING

We open the window
as wide as possible
to hear bird song.

You meet new experiences with caution.

It isn't surprising that you're
suspicious of anything new,

until you learn how fruitful
these new things can be.

And where they can take us.

Seeing how we've changed.

Stumbling on together.

Francis, thank you for sharing all
your happiness and oranges.

And to

Emil
Elva
Billy
Kezzy
Sena
Ira
Rex
Roland
Arthur
Cosmo
Willow
Maya
Sol
Frieda
Jago
Pearl

And all the marvellous babies
who arrived with us at
this very strange time.

For you this is only the very first chapter.